FINDING *our* WAY *to* GOD

A Pilgrimage with the Psalms

Harvey A. Stob

CRC Publications
Grand Rapids, Michigan

Printed in the United States of America on recycled paper. ♻

Library of Congress Cataloging-in-Publication Data

Stob, Harvey A., 1944-

Finding our way to God: a pilgrimage with the Psalms/Harvey A. Stob

p. cm.

ISBN 1-56212-130-8 (alk. paper)

1. Bible. O.T. Psalm—Meditations. I. Title.

BS1445.S6S75 1995

223'.206—dc20 95-33979

CIP

10 9 8 7 6 5 4 3 2 1

CONTENTS

PREFACE

The drama of our human life has three acts: our being with God, our leaving God, and our returning to God. Acts 1 and 2 have already been written and played—without us and before our time. Act 3, however, is still being written and played as we live it and according to how we live it. Our decisions and our actions determine its final end.

The possibility of Act 3 ending well rests on the coming of Jesus, who invites us to follow him back to God and back to life. The good news of Jesus is that God has made our return possible. We, however, must undertake the journey willingly and decisively, following Jesus back to God's presence.

This six-session study for small groups maps out the steps of that journey. It is offered with the prayer that this may help you return to God, the source and the radiance of our life.

Harvey A. Stob

Gracious God, may your Word be the truth by which we live;
may your Spirit be the power with which we live;
may your honor and your glory be the goals for which we live. Amen.

INTRODUCTION

These materials have been developed for the use of small groups of Christian believers who wish to grow spiritually.

You may consider that description redundant, because everyone who is a believer should, of course, wish to grow spiritually. Didn't the apostle Paul urge us all to "become mature" and "in all things grow up into . . . Christ" (Eph. 4:13, 15)?

Still, although all believers may wish to become better Christians, to follow Jesus in their style of living, to draw closer to God through prayer, meditation, and Scripture reading, and to submit themselves more fully to the influence and guidance of the Holy Spirit, not all are willing to be guided by other believers in the formation of their spiritual lives. Not all are willing to join a small group whose declared purpose is to turn from the interests and values of this world and to immerse themselves in spiritual matters. And these materials are developed for believers who have such a willingness and purpose.

Note well that we are not talking about people who are looking for some spirit hidden within their own hearts, some spiritual dimension of their own existence, or some nature spirit of the earth. That is a pursuit characteristic of New Age religiosity and its mentors. We are, rather, talking about the Spirit of God who makes our own spirits alive (Rom. 8:9-10). Any and all spiritual formation that takes place among us is by and through the Holy Spirit of God.

Why in Small Groups?

What are the advantages of using these materials in a small group, that is, with two to fourteen other people? Couldn't this be done alone, in the solitude of one's own room, or in a broader church community? Certainly. But meeting, studying, and discussing with a small group offer certain benefits.

Some of these benefits are fairly general. A small group provides us the community support we all need. It permits us to develop deep and meaningful relationships with people who are of like mind and spirit. It provides a healthy intimacy.

Other benefits of working in a small group are specifically related to dealing with spiritual formation materials. It is easy to deceive ourselves about where we are in spiritual matters. Being in a group helps keep us honest, because someone in the group is likely to detect any fraud or pretence. It makes us accountable. If we dedicate ourselves to certain new spiritual practices (such as meditating and praying for a certain length of time each day), someone else will know whether or not we are doing what we promised to do. A small group can also provide encouragement and the prayerful support of others on the same spiritual journey. And we can learn from each other's advances and setbacks.

How to Use These Materials

Every member of your group—or every couple within your group—should have a copy of this book. However, we have left considerable flexibility for how your group and your leader may wish to use these materials.

Each of the six sessions in this booklet is organized into four parts. *Where are we?* introduces the subject and invites you to reflect on it personally and discuss it with your group. *Where are we going?* permits you to study, think about, meditate on, and talk about the Scripture passages and related materials being presented. *What do we say to God?* encourages your group to make time to speak to God about what you have learned. *What do we do next?* points out ways to get ready for the next group session.

You will notice that most of what follows is divided into two columns. The larger, left-hand column contains materials meant to be read by group members. How these are read may vary from group to group and from session to session. Some groups may wish to read them before the group meeting. Others may wish to read them silently, section by section, during the session. Still others may wish to have them read aloud, either by one or several persons in the group. Use whatever method works best for you.

Regardless of how these materials are used, they should always be read slowly, thoughtfully, and meditatively. They are not facts for memorizing or scientific observations for critiquing. They are thoughts from and for the heart. Be sure they are read in that way.

The smaller, right-hand column has suggestions for group activities, questions for discussion, and so on. You should feel free to choose from among these or to substitute your own ideas or questions.

Forty-five minutes is the bare minimum you will need for each session; try to allow an hour or more. Rushing through the readings, questions, and discussions will defeat the purpose of these materials. A spiritual journey cannot be rushed. It requires time to absorb, time to contemplate, time to weigh our own experiences and thoughts, and time to take the requisite steps.

Such a spiritual journey also requires intimacy within the small group. If you are a new group, that will take time to develop. The setting of your meeting will make a difference. If possible, meet in someone's home, sitting in a comfortable circle, where everyone can see each other and talk face to face.

Your small group may already have a leader. If not, someone is needed to direct the readings and pace the discussions. Whoever serves as leader should be a full and equal participant in the journey—a facilitator rather than a lecturer. Following Jesus' directive, this leader should be the servant of the group, yet should be given the honor and attention due to those who serve among us.

Songs of Ascents

This book presents for your reflection and spiritual guidance a group of psalms (120-134) called the *Songs of Ascents,* or the *Book of Pilgrim Songs.* Most scholars agree that these ascents were to Jerusalem, to Mount Zion, and to the temple where God was uniquely present. The pilgrimages in which these songs were used were journeys to the great, annual religious festivals in worship of God.

The Jews came eagerly to these pilgrim trips because these journeys brought them into the very presence of their God. They came to make confessions, to receive forgiveness, to pay their vows, to make resolutions, and to receive meaning for their lives. These journeys to the sanctuary were highly charged with spiritual significance. Accordingly, the words of these songs were part of the observance and expressed what was going on in the pilgrimages. The songs served as a handbook of devotions for the pilgrims, leading their spirits into the divine presence. They can serve us in the same way.

This collection of psalms is not a random one. The order and progression will become obvious as our study advances. Please notice the smaller sets of psalms within the larger collection. Psalms 120 through 123 set the journey to God in motion and get it on track. Psalms 124 through 128 are songs sung on the road—campfire songs sung at the end of a day's travel. Psalms 129 through 131 are spiritually crucial, for in these we see the progress of the pilgrimage suddenly threatened. Psalms 132 through 134 prepare us for entering into the presence of God, the goal and the joy of our journey.

"Everyman is as holy as he really wants to be."
A. W. Tozer, *Man: The Dwelling Place of God,* p. 40

SESSION 1

THE JOURNEY

Where are we?

In Revelation 2:1-7, Jesus commends his church in Ephesus for her activity (v. 2), her orthodoxy (v. 2), and her perseverance (v. 3). He judges her, however, for having forsaken her first love (v. 4). Did this church exchange her "first love" for another, or was she simply no longer in love? How does a church stay in love with God?

PSALM 63:1-8

O God, you are my God,
earnestly I seek you;
my soul thirsts for you,
my body longs for you,
in a dry and weary land
where there is no water.

I have seen you in the sanctuary
and beheld your power and your glory.
Because your love is better than life,
my lips will glorify you.
I will praise you as long as I live,
and in your name I will lift up my hands.
My soul will be satisfied as with the richest of foods;
with singing lips my mouth will praise you.
On my bed I remember you;
I think of you through the watches of the night.
Because you are my help,
I sing in the shadow of your wings.
My soul clings to you (author's trans.);
your right hand upholds me.

Talk about your love of God. How do you perceive it? As a feeling? As a longing? As a resolve? As a trust? What can/should you do to "stay in love with God"?

Where are we going?

The journey before us will be demanding and exhilarating. In Psalm 63, we see its breathtaking scope. The journey is mapped out in short phrases, one following the other, each reaching a plateau higher and more glorious than the one before it.

Note the three references to "soul" in Psalm 63. Do you see a movement higher in each succeeding reference?

Ground Level

"O God . . ." Our journey begins here, with a glance toward God. We first sense that there is a God, that God exists. As we grew up, we heard our parents speak about God. We heard God mentioned in church and in Sunday school. The idea of a God existing somewhere is not a strange idea to us. Here's where we begin.

"O God . . ." is our starting point. From here we look up and see God above and ahead of us. God is out there.

Do you remember when you first became aware of God? Did that start you on the way to God, or did it turn you away?

The First Plateau

"O God . . ." first. "You are my God," next. An entire spiritual universe lies between those two phrases. How do I travel from one to the other? How do I cross the infinite space that lies between my knowing that there is a God and knowing that the God who *is,* is *my* God. How do I help my children travel that enormous spiritual distance from hearing about their parents' God to calling this majestic being "my God"?

"O God/you are my God. . . ." Think of the distance between those two phrases. Can anyone travel it? Not you. Not I. This second phrase will have no real meaning unless and until God desires to be our God and allows us say "my God." We could say "my God" or "our God" all we wish, but for that to mean anything at all, God has to be our God in deed and in fact.

■

Was there a time when you could not say, meaningfully, "my God" or "our God"? Recall that time and how you felt toward God then.

"O God . . ., O God . . ., O God . . .!" We can repeat that phrase a thousand times. Repeat it plaintively, repeat it wishfully, or repeat it desperately. "O God . . ., O God . . ., O God . . .!" It can come from deep within our hearts. But it remains, always, our word, our shout, our human cry, rising from our human situation.

This second phrase, radically profound and daring, "You are my God," is not ours. Not in the sense that it comes from us. There is no way that we would dare make the claim that this phrase makes if God had not first allowed us to say it.

"You are *my* God!" What an extravagant thing for us to be able to say! "You, the God of Abraham, Isaac, and Jacob; you, the God of Moses, David, and the prophets; you are my God too! You are for me as you were for them. You demand of me what you demanded of them. You are my God!"

Can this phrase be true? Can you say it and have its truth ring throughout all time and all space? Yes! "Praise be to the God and Father of our Lord Jesus Christ . . . . For he chose us in him . . . to be holy and blameless in his sight. In love he predestined us to be adopted . . . through Jesus Christ . . . " (Eph. 1:3-5).

Why and how does God allow this?
How did God arrange this adoption?

■

The God who *is* there is there for you and me! God, the almighty, the magnificent, the gracious God is my God!

Our spiritual journey begins when we go from "O God" to "You are my God." Anyone can and everyone does say "O God!" Anybody and everybody can be at the starting point. But staying there doesn't make a journey. The journey is underway when we reach the first plateau, saying, "You are my God . . .!"

Are you on this first plateau?
Can you truly say "my God"?

The Second Plateau

"O God, you are my God, earnestly I seek you . . . ." The God who *is*, is my God. Not in the sense of being my personal god. Not a god I keep in a drawer somewhere and take out when I need a little help. God is never "ours" in the sense that we own or control him or have any hold on him whatsoever. If we owned God, we wouldn't have to seek him. If we controlled God, we would never have to look for him.

"O God, you are my God, earnestly I seek you . . . ." Why should we seek God? We seek what we do not have. But we've already seen that God has come to us, so it's not as if we don't have him.

"Earnestly I seek you." But what is it that we seek? God's advice? Yes. God's forgiveness? Of course. God's favor? Certainly. God's will for our lives? That too. But listen to what the psalmist says. See where the psalmist wants to take us.

"Earnestly I seek you!" the psalmist says, with nothing further added. It is God himself whom the psalmist seeks. Not something from God, but God's self. He doesn't want to tell God something; he simply (!) wants to be in the divine presence, to be with God. "I seek *you*."

This is the language of love. We may seek God for all sorts of legitimate reasons. But here the poet's only desire is for God himself. Such seeking is born of love. As one writer has noted, "To love God without demand or without measure, in and for Himself—this is Love."

Evelyn Underhill, *Anthology of the Love of God*, p. 30

■

How often do you turn to God or pray because you want something? How often do you turn to him or pray simply because you want to be in God's presence?

"Love the Lord your God with all your heart and with all your soul and with all your mind" (Matt. 22:37). The God who is love invites us, "come with me" (Song of Songs 2:10).

"You will seek me and find me when you seek me with all your heart" (Jer. 29:13). Seeking God requires a desire to be in God's presence and to enjoy his company.

To earnestly seek God means that we are making every attempt to be with him. Prayer, Bible reading, meditation, talking with God about ourselves, asking about God, listening to God—all these can be such attempts. God is a person and so are we. People get to know each other only when they open themselves to each other, and people get to love each other only when they listen in love to what is in the other's heart. God invites us to do this with him.

"O God, you are my God, earnestly I seek you."

"Seek and you shall find!" Jesus promised.

Can the love of God be commanded? Invited? Encouraged? Strengthened?

■

Philosopher Blaise Pascal once observed that there are three types of people:

- those who do not seek God and therefore haven't found him;
- those who are seeking God but haven't found him yet;
- and those who sought God and have found him indeed.

Jesus promised that everyone in the second category will someday be in the third. To seek God is to find him.

Our journey isn't over. There are higher, more glorious plateaus yet to reach.

Christian philosopher Peter Kreeft observed that "fear of the Lord may be the beginning of wisdom, but love of the Lord is wisdom's end" (*Yes or No?*, p. 170). Is this true?

The Third Plateau

"O God, you are my God, earnestly I seek you; my soul thirsts for you . . . ."

Seeking is something conscious, active, and voluntary. To thirst is another matter. Thirsting is involuntary and signals that something necessary for life is missing and needed. We thirst because our bodies send our brains a message: "Drink some water." If that message is not answered soon, it will grow louder and louder. Ignored too long, it will go away.

"My soul thirsts for you . . ." is a stage on our spiritual journey where we cannot do without God, where he has become such a vital part of our lives that our souls cry out when, for a short time, God is absent from our thinking, talking, and feeling. We may get a taste of this when we have to miss worship services for a while or when, for some reason, we can't have our daily devotions. Our souls become thirsty. Something necessary for life—God—is missing.

Do you thirst for God? When? What satisfies that thirst?

The Fourth Plateau

This thirst for God takes us quickly to the next plateau: *"Your love, O God, is better than life!"* (v. 3).

Life is pretty good for most of us. Lots of nice things to do. Interesting places to go. Attractive prizes to reach for. But to know the love of God, to bask in the steadfast love of God, to be embraced by the love of God—there is nothing in this life to match that!

"Your love is better than life," says the psalmist. To know the value of God's love is to know the value of all other things. To know the great value of Christ's love is to know the lesser value of whatever money, power, or prestige this life offers.

"Your love is better than life." This is the place on our journey where decisions are easily made, where priorities are automatically set. Here there are few sacrifices, for who would consider it a sacrifice to give up a lesser thing for a greater? And the love of God exceeds in beauty and value all else that we might ever have or enjoy.

The Summit

Our destination is now before us. We have looked to God. We have sought him earnestly. We have thirsted for God. We have been embraced by his love. And now we're there. We are at a place where, as verse 8 says, "I stay close to you and your right hand upholds me."

Do you remember your two-year-old clinging to your leg? And how you, reaching down with your hand, lifted your child up? How good it felt to be able to do that, and how secure your child felt being allowed to cling in that way.

I don't know if the psalmist had such a memory in mind when he wrote verse 8, but the safety, the love, and the security expressed in the psalm are something like that memory. We are now clinging to God, not letting him go, not letting him out of our sight. And God is picking us up, carrying us in his arms, protecting us, caring for us. We are with him, in constant, close communion.

What, apart from God, do you value most highly in life? Would you willingly sacrifice it for the sake of God's love?

What do we say to God?

O God, I love thee, I love thee—
Not out of hope of heaven for me
Nor fearing not to love and be
In the everlasting burning
Thou, thou, my Jesus, after me
Didst reach thine arms out dying,
For my sake sufferedst nails and lance,
Mocked and marred countenance,
Sorrows passing number,
Sweat and care and cumber,
Yea and death, and this from me,
And thou couldst see me sinning:
Then I, why should not I love thee,

Lady Julian of Norwich prayed for three wounds: the wound of true contrition, the wound of kind compassion, and the wound of earnest longing for God. Why does she call them "wounds," and why should you pray to receive them?

Revelations of Divine Love, p. 339

Jesu so much in love with me?
Not for heaven's sake; not to be
Out of hell by loving thee;
Not for any gains I see;
But just the way that thou didst me
I do love and I will love thee:
What must I love thee, Lord, for then?—
For being my king and God. Amen.

Gerard Manley Hopkins, from
The HarperCollins Book of Prayers, p. 204

Together, pray this prayer by Hopkins. Follow this with a time of prayer focusing on God's love for us and our love in response.

What do we do next?

The next session will focus on our preparation for the journey. Read and meditate on Psalm 120. Imagine yourself preparing for a spiritual pilgrimage and think of what preparations you should make for that journey.

"How can the Holy Ghost fill your soul when it's full of trash?" the priest roared. "The Holy Ghost will not come until you see yourself as you are—a lazy, ignorant, conceited youth!" he said, pounding his fist on the little bedside table.

Flannery O'Connor, *The Enduring Chill*

SESSION 2

PREPARATION

Where are we?

Before we can begin our journey into God's presence, we must recognize how far we need to travel. How do we come to know that? Given our human nature, most often it is not goodness but weariness that leads us to such recognition.

When God at first made man,
Having a glass of blessings standing by,
"Let us" (said he) "pour on him all we can;
Let the world's riches, which dispersed lie,
Contract into a span."

So strength first made a way;
Then beauty flow'd, then wisdom, honour, pleasure.
When almost all was out, God made a stay,
Perceiving that alone of all his treasure
Rest in the bottom lay.

"For if I should" (said he)
"Bestow this jewel also on my creature,
He would adore my gifts instead of me,
And rest in Nature, not the God of Nature
So both should losers be.

"Yet let him keep the rest,
But keep them with repining restlessness;
Let him be rich and weary, that at least,

If goodness lead him not, yet weariness
May toss him to my breast."

George Herbert, "The Pulley"

Weariness is a blessing when we are courageous enough to receive it as God's gift. Lacking that courage, we struggle against our restlessness rather than pass through it, as if it were a door, to God.

Blaise Pascal said that "what people want is not the easy peaceful life that allows us to think of our unhappy condition . . . but the agitation that takes our mind off it and diverts us" (*Pensees*, p. 173).

Have you ever experienced weariness as a blessing? Describe that experience.

■

Weariness points us to God, while diversion literally turns us away from God. Created to marvel at the beauty and diversity of our beings and our worlds, we are turned to worldly things and encouraged to buy, to possess, and to devour them.

Lovingly created to receive our Maker's love, our hearts are told that other loves are as fulfilling.

Created to hear, to learn, and to acknowledge that we have been loved into existence, loved into freedom, loved so that we might enter love, we are diverted, turned away. And that diversion is so easily accomplished and so welcome to us.

Meditate silently for a few minutes on these observations.

PSALM 120

I call on the Lord in my distress,
and he answers me.
Save me, O Lord, from lying lips
and from deceitful tongues.

What will he do to you,
and what more besides, O deceitful tongue?
He will punish you with a warrior's sharp arrows,
with burning coals of the broom tree.

Woe to me that I dwell in Meshech,
that I live among the tents of Kedar!
Too long have I lived
among those who hate peace.
I am a man of peace;
but when I speak, they are for war.

Where are we going?

"To the Lord, in my distress, I cry" (author's translation). So begins Psalm 120, the first of the *Songs of Ascents.* These are pilgrim songs, songs for the road, melodies to be sung on our way to the presence of God. The song will be full and harmonious at journey's end, but it is singular, discordant, and lonely here at the beginning: "To the Lord, in my distress, I cry."

Have you experienced distress that made you cry to God? Describe that experience.

Diversions

The cause of the poet's distress does not seem to be physical. He suffers no illness and no injury. Rather, his distress comes from his weariness, which he has recognized and which has been made sharp and heavy by the diversions all around him.

"Lord, save my soul from lips that lie, from tongues that deceive" (author's translation). Anything and everything that diverts our soul's attention from God deceives us. Diversions are lies because they seek to put ideas, things, or people at the center of our souls where only God belongs. "Lord, save my soul . . . ."

The word we speak when our diversions are exposed is "woe," a painful exclamation not often heard today. But when the lies we once accepted are recognized as such, "woe" is the only appropriate response. It is appropriate not only because we now see the falseness of one reality but also because we have not yet grasped the truth of the other reality. We have been shaken loose from false reality, but we are not yet fully attached to God, the true reality. And that is why we are in distress; that is why we cry out.

"Woe to me . . ." is the first cry of any pilgrim, for she sees where she is and, in distress, yearns to be somewhere else. "Woe to me that I dwell in Meshech, that I live among the tents of Kedar."

Meshech and Kedar are names of different tribes. Meshech was a far-off tribe, thousands of miles north of Palestine in what is now southern Russia. On the fringe of civilization, it was very far from Jerusalem, where God dwelt.

What lies were spoken there that kept the people of Meshech from recognizing their great distance from God? The lie that knowledge can give us mastery of the world? The lie that God is within us and we can find him conveniently there?

What diversions in your life keep you from looking to God? Sports? Work? Degrees and careers? So many prizes to win? "Woe to me that I dwell in Meshech!"

■

What is the main diversion in your life? Your work? Your family? Sports? Entertainment? Church life? How may any or all of these divert you from God and become lies?

Kedar is the name of a tribe of Bedouins who lived along the desert border of Israel. They had the reputation of being a barbaric, savage people. Their lives, too, were built upon lies—lies that denied the justice of God; lies that denied the obligation to love their neighbors; lies that denied peace and chose war.

What diversions here among the tents of Kedar keep us from looking to God? The greatest diversion of them all: that we are God and that our goals are good, our reasons sufficient, and our desires right. And we pitch our gold and silver tents in the sand.

What finally pierces our lies and our diversions here in this desert? What breaks through the diversions and forces us to face the distance between ourselves and God? Someone else's power, more savage than our own. An illness that our powers cannot combat. Tragedy.

Failure. Weariness. Grace. "Woe to me that I live among the tents of Kedar."

Thank God for the word "woe." It is the word of recognition, awareness, and discomfort. And if we are willing to accept this discomfort, we might then be prepared to find the blessing that true comfort waits to give us.

We must, however, allow that discomfort to go deep into our souls so that we are shaken loose not only from false gods around us but also from every false god within us. Distress must lead to detachment if we pilgrims are going to travel any distance toward God.

Detachment

Detachment is a cross already too heavy for many people to bear today. We not only grow attached to things naturally, but we are also invited and encouraged continually to attach our hearts to physical things (and to causes, and to people). We are *never* told that we have more things than we need. We are *ever* told that we do not have enough. Always there is something more, something new that we must not be without, something we should acquire.

Jesus said, "If anyone would come after me, he must deny himself and take up his cross and follow me" (Matt. 16:24). Is there a necessary progression from denying one's self, to taking up one's cross, to following Jesus? Can you do the last without doing the first two? Where are you on this path?

And yet detachment is what Jesus expects of us. No, detachment is what Jesus demands of us. It is a requirement of discipleship. "Any of you who does not give up everything he has cannot be my disciple" (Luke 14:33).

When Jesus' disciples attempted to keep little children from coming to him, Jesus protested and welcomed the children. He urged his followers to become like them. "I tell you the truth," he said, "anyone who will not receive the kingdom of God like a little child will never enter it" (Mark 10:15). The kingdom can only be received—never acquired or gained. Children receive well.

Jesus' disciples did not attempt to keep a wealthy man from him. Yet this was a man Jesus could not welcome as a disciple, for he wasn't at all like a child. He wanted to know what he could do in order to gain eternal life. Because we can only receive—never gain—that life, he had to become one who could receive. To become that, he had to detach himself from what he had. "'Go, sell everything you have and give to the poor, and you will have treasure in heaven. Then come, follow me.' At this the man's face fell. He went away sad, because he had great wealth" (Mark 10:21-22). He could not attach himself to Jesus because he could not first detach himself from his possessions.

■

"Anyone aspiring to intimacy with God must learn to detach his heart from things not God" (T. Dubay, *Faith Within*, p. 107). What might those things be? How do you learn to detach your heart from things, not God?

Abraham was the first to be called to the side of God. The first word spoken to him—the word that comes first to us all—was "leave" (Gen. 12:1). Detach yourself from your homeland, from your clan, and from your family, the Lord said to Abraham. Detach . . . and go. First detach, then go.

And Abraham detached himself. He "left, as the Lord had told him" (Gen. 12:4). How pleased the Lord must have been! Not that all the needed detachment was completed, however. Abraham's beginning was exemplary, but it was only a beginning. A further detachment still had to be made, and it would be a far more difficult one. That occurred when God told Abraham to detach himself from his son, Isaac (Gen. 22).

Nothing attaches us to the earth more than our children. God knows that. The Lord's requirements of Abraham unfold in successive phrases, building in severity to the climactic test: "Take your son, your only son Isaac, whom you love . . . sacrifice him!" (Gen. 22:2).

There is only one possible explanation for Abraham's willingness to detach himself from his beloved son: that Abraham was now completely attached to God. And when he showed himself to be so attached, he received Isaac back.

We are often told that Abraham's test is unique, that God would never test us in the same way. But God does. Jesus said, "If anyone comes to me and does not hate his father and mother, his wife and children, his brothers and sisters—yes, even his own life—he cannot be my disciple" (Luke 14:26). Detachment.

"Blessed are the poor in spirit" (Matt. 5:3). Detachment.

Of course, in all of this we are only disciples, following and learning from our master, "Who, being in very nature God, did not consider equality with God something to be grasped, but made himself nothing . . ." (Phil. 2:6).

God detached for us. We detach for God.

Detachment doesn't mean that you take no pleasure in the things God has created but only that you see and use them for the reasons God created them. Then your pleasure in them will be pure.

What concretely can you do to detach for God?

What do we say to God?

> *Receive, O Lord, all my freedom, my memory, my understanding, and my will. All that I have or cherish, you have given. I return it all to you that it may be guided by your will. Only your love and grace I ask. With these I am rich and ask for nothing more.*
>
> Ignatius of Loyola, from Evelyn Underhill, *The Ways of the Spirit*, p. 122

What do we do next?

Session 3 begins your departure on the spiritual journey. Read Psalms 121, 122, and 123 as often you are able, meditating on them after each reading. Imagine this coming pilgrimage. Consider how long, how difficult, and how dangerous it may be, and where it may take you. Map in your mind's eye the direction and shape of this coming journey.

Use Ignatius's words as an opening prayer for a period spent in confessing your diversions and promising your detachment from these things.

My unassisted heart is barren clay,
That of its native self can nothing feed:
Of good and pious works Thou art the seed,
That quickens only where Thou sayest it may:
Unless Thou show to us Thine own true way
No man can find it: Father! Thou must lead.

Michelangelo (from A. W. Tozer, *The Pursuit of God*, p. 67)

SESSION 3

DEPARTURE

Where are we?

Every journey has a destination, a point of departure, and a distance to be traveled. Once the destination has been determined and the departure made, the distance to be traveled becomes our major concern. Is it short or long, easy or hard, safe or dangerous?

The journey to the presence of God is generally neither short nor easy nor safe. Forces within and without are hostile to our journey's success. Between the land of slavery and the promised land lies a desert. And as our pilgrim ancestors, the children of Israel, discovered, in the heat of the desert our journey is in jeopardy.

Psalms 121, 122, and 123 face the distance, see the desert, and recognize the danger. They take its measure and set us as pilgrims rightly on our way.

What fears do you have about this spiritual journey? Does it appear to be a hard and dangerous desert pilgrimage?

Where are we going?

PSALM 121

I lift up my eyes to the hills—
where does my help come from?
My help comes from the LORD,
the Maker of heaven and earth.

He will not let your foot slip—
he who watches over you will not slumber;
indeed, he who watches over Israel
will neither slumber nor sleep.

The LORD *watches over you—*
the LORD *is your shade at your right hand;*
the sun will not harm you by day,
nor the moon by night.

The LORD *will keep you from all harm—*
he will watch over your life;
the LORD *will watch over your coming and going*
both now and forevermore.

With the writer of Psalm 121 we lift up our eyes. This is necessary. Our journey requires that we look up. But we must be sure to lift up our eyes all the way.

The pilgrim first looks up but does not look high enough. He sees the hills and becomes anxious; she gazes on the hills and is filled with concern.

Every pilgrim going to Jerusalem had to face the geographic reality of these hills. They represented real physical hardship—rocks and ravines and narrow paths; this journey was not going to be easy. The hills also held the threat of physical danger—thieves and wild beasts would be hiding there; the journey was never safe.

The hills ahead are spiritual realities as well, formidable ones that we each recognize. "I lift up my eyes to the hills—where does my help come from?" Hear the anxiety expressed in these words. Who will help us ascend these hills, survive their dangers, and reach our destination on their other side?

List the very real hardships and dangers, both physical and spiritual, that lie ahead on your journey.

Crisis

The first crisis that the Israelites faced was not how they might free themselves from Egyptian oppression. The Lord would take care of that. Their first great crisis was how they would survive the desert that lay between them and the promised land. More specifically, who would go with them into the desert and enable them to survive it?

When Moses did not return from his mountaintop meeting with the Lord as quickly as they thought he should, the pilgrim people insisted that other gods be readied. "Come," they said to Aaron, "make us gods who will go before us" (Ex. 32:1). Gods were needed, for the journey ahead was filled with peril. If one god isn't available, thought the Israelites, others should be found.

The Lord, outraged, was ready to let them and their new gods go into the desert without him (Ex. 33:1-3). But Moses courageously pleaded, "If your Presence does not go with us, do not send us up from here" (Ex. 33:15).

Moses knew that before them lay a desert, a waterless, foodless, inhospitable stretch of land with dangerous hills. Moses knew that if the Lord did not accompany them, it would be better not to risk the journey. Better to perish in the foothills than to travel without the Lord. Better to call off the journey than to reach any destination without the Lord being there too.

"I lift up my eyes to the hills—where does my help come from?" Where will our help come from?

■

New Age spirituality offers various gurus to guide people on their spiritual journey. How are they like the golden calf of the Israelites?

All pilgrims know that help is needed on our journey to God's presence. We need help, for the desert is very dry and the hills are very high. Like the writer of Psalm 121, we are concerned about three dangers: slipping (vv. 3-4), being vulnerable to the elements (vv. 5-6), and being touched by evil (v. 7).

In the Psalms, the phrase "foot slipping" normally has a moral connotation. The prosperity of the wicked and the successes of their endeavors may cause our feet to slip (Ps. 73:2). Or our own righteous ways may not bring outward blessings, and the inward blessings may not satisfy us. If so, our feet may slip. Out of weakness, out of envy, out of desire, out of being tired with trying to live rightly, we may slip off God's path (Ps. 17:5). We may rebel against God's ways (Ps. 37:31).

Moral failure stops every spiritual pilgrimage. If we fail morally, we will be left lying disabled at the side of the road. Then from where will our help come?

Spend a few moments, silently, remembering how your feet have slipped in the past.

■

The sun exhausts us during the day, the moon maddens us during the night (*lunatic* come from *luna*, Latin for moon). Diseases—cancers and strokes, depressions and anxieties—can strike and confuse us, making us forget our destination. From where will our help come?

Evil thoughts and evil people tell us there is no promised land on the far side of the desert. They ridicule our peculiar ways and think our moral rules are quaint. They prey on our love and then mock the goodness of our hearts. They seek to take our Savior away, hiding him in the myths of ancient fantasy. They rob us of our hope and insist that we stand with them, alone, in the hot and waterless desert.

"I lift up my eyes to the hills—where does my help come from? My help comes from the Lord, the maker of heaven and earth." The Lord is the maker of every desert and every hill.

Five times in this psalm God is referred to by his personal name *Yahweh* (*Lord* in the NIV). Six times he is called our keeper (in Hebrew, one word means both "watches over" and "keeps"). At the beginning of the pilgrimage, the psalmist recognizes that the central issue is not the problems and difficulties we will encounter but rather who goes with us on the way.

Deep in the hills or far off in the desert, the Lord travels at our side. The God who is the beginning (he bids us come) and the end (he is our goal) is with us also in the middle. God is present at the departure, at the destination, and on the long trip in between. We can travel with utmost confidence, because we know from where our help will come.

How can you be sure the Lord goes with you into the desert? Is this strictly a matter of faith? What, if anything, can you do to ensure the Lord's presence?

PSALM 122

I rejoiced with those who said to me,
"Let us go to the house of the LORD."
Our feet are standing
in your gates, O Jerusalem.

Jerusalem is built like a city
that is closely compacted together.
That is where the tribes go up,
the tribes of the LORD,
to praise the name of the LORD
according to the statute given to Israel.
There the thrones for judgment stand,
the thrones of the house of David.

Pray for the peace of Jerusalem:
"May those who love you be secure.
May there be peace within your walls
and security within your citadels."
For the sake of my brothers and friends,
I will say, "Peace be within you."
For the sake of the house of the LORD our God,
I will seek your prosperity.

God loves each of us (Rom. 1:7). Love binds two hearts together so that only the lover and the beloved truly know their particular love. God loves each of us singularly and therefore uniquely. "Why else were individuals created, but that God, loving all infinitely, should love each differently?" wrote C. S. Lewis in one of his books.

You cannot exhaustively express to me your love for God and God's love for you. That love is meant to be enjoyed by the two of you.

Each of us is called by God to be holy, to be a saint. With our distinctive personalities, abilities, and interests, we each become a saint of different hues, a loving singer of different lines. We are each required to carry a particular cross. That cross is ours because it is laid on our shoulders in the place where we are and for the time it is given.

Loved by God, called to be saints, given a cross as the means to fulfill that calling, each of us journeys over the hills with individual resolve. I am loved, and therefore I go to be with the One who loves me. You are called, and therefore you pick up your cross and fall in behind Jesus.

This means that each of us is a disciple individually. But not a disciple alone.

God did not observe that Adam was lonely in the Garden Eden but that he was alone. Loneliness is a vertical condition of human existence in which no "Thou" is in contact with a human "I." Aloneness is a horizontal condition based on distance from other people. We can be in a crowd and suffer acute loneliness; we also can be alone and not be lonely at all.

No one loved by God is ever lonely, not even in his or her most alone moment—death. Even there, especially there, our Lord is with us.

What is the distinction between being lonely and being alone? Have you ever experienced being alone but not lonely?

"I Believe in the Communion of Saints"

We who are loved by God are not lonely, and we are not alone either. We have heard God's bidding and have begun our journey to his presence—we are given the gift of the communion of saints. "I rejoiced with those who said to me, 'Let us . . . .'" Notice the *us*. Together, one with the other, one for the other, "Let us go to the house of the LORD."

The communion of saints does not and cannot supplant our personal communion with God. We must not think of it as a substitute for our communion with Christ. And it isn't meant to keep us from being lonely—God gives himself to us for that. Rather, the communion of saints keeps us from being alone. And that is a true gift indeed.

We are "surrounded by . . . a great cloud of witnesses" (Heb. 12:1). These are the saints, individually called yet forming together a band of witnesses. They are not witnesses *of* us, watching what we do. Instead, they are witnesses *to* us.

Each of these saints has felt the stirring of God's love. Each has heard God's call to love him in return. Far into their desert crossings, deep into their hill journeys (see how they suffered according to Hebrews 11!), each has found God to be present, to be faithful to his promises, and at the end, to embrace their coming with his love.

They surround us to tell us that it is true: that God is love; that in Jesus there is life; that the desert is not limitless; that the hills have their boundaries; and that God goes with us there.

Martin Luther recovered the biblical truth that all believers are priests, that each of us has access through Jesus Christ to God's forgiveness, love, and life. We do not have to find some other person to bring us to God.

Yet the priesthood of all believers also means that each of us is a priest to the other. You call me to repentance; I encourage you to remain faithful to God. You remind me of God's love; I help you understand what God's will is. The communion of saints means that we walk with other pilgrims into the hills and deserts, on our way together to God.

Have others helped you on your journey? Give an example of such help.

PSALM 123

I lift up my eyes to you,
to you whose throne is in the heaven.
As the eyes of slaves look to the hand of their master,
as the eyes of a maid look to the hand of her mistress,
so our eyes look to the LORD our God,
till he shows us his mercy.

Have mercy on us, O LORD, have mercy on us,
for we have endured much contempt.
We have endured much ridicule from the proud,
much contempt from the arrogant.

When "I lift up my eyes to the hills" (Ps. 121), I become anxious about my life and my journey. But having been assured that the Maker of every hill watches over and cares for me, having been given the gift of the communion of saints, I now lift my eyes higher.

"To you I lift up my eyes, to you whose throne is in heaven" (author's translation). "To you . . . " Not to blind fate, not to capricious fortune, not to some infinite expanse of personless being, but "to you . . . ." A "Thou" is on the throne in heaven, a master and a mistress to whom you and I, slaves and maids, may look.

There is a great, yet wonderful, tension, daring and naive, expressed in Psalm 123. We lift up our eyes and look directly at God. Yet we do not do this as an equal. Rather, as a servant looks to a master or a maid to a mistress, as a dependent duty-bound to do the master's or mistress's will, so we presume to look at our God "till he shows us his mercy." In love, God allows us to do this!

"Faith is the gaze of a soul upon a saving God."

"When we lift our inward eyes to gaze upon God we are sure to meet friendly eyes gazing back at us . . . ."

Discuss one or both of the following quotes in the left column from A. W. Tozer, *The Pursuit of God,* p. 92:

What do we say to God?

> *We know, O God, that we must change if we are to see Thy face: none but the holy can see Thee. O support us as we proceed in this great, awful, happy change, with the grace of Thine unchangeableness. Let us day by day be molded by Thee and be changed from glory to glory by ever looking towards Thee and ever leaning on Thy strength.*
>
> John Henry Newman (from Evelyn Underhill, *The Ways of the Spirit*, p. 89)

What do we do next?

Your next session will be studying five *Songs of Ascents,* Psalms 124 through 128. In these psalms, the pilgrims are on their way to Jerusalem, climbing slowly up to God's dwelling place. Read these five psalms, meditating on each. Imagine yourself, with your fellow pilgrims, camped for the night and singing these songs around the campfire. What emotions are aroused in you and what thoughts come to mind as you sing these songs?

Together, say this prayer by John Henry Newman. Follow it with thanks to God for loving and calling you and for providing fellow saints who encourage and guide you on your spiritual journey.

You who ride on white donkeys, sitting on your saddle blankets, and you who walk along the road, consider the voice of the singers at the watering places. . . .

Judges 5:10

SESSION 4

ON THE WAY

Where are we?

The journey to the full presence of God, being neither short nor easy, requires endurance. Our eyes are now fixed on God, our destination, and our hearts will not rest until we are with him.

Originally, we set out one by one. But now, gratefully, we find ourselves traveling in the company of others, both those who have traveled this way before and those who are traveling it now. With these fellow travelers (past and present) we speak. From them, we receive encouragement. With them, we continue on the way. Endurance for this journey comes both from the Spirit of our God and from the words of our companions.

Psalms 124-128 are travel songs sung by saints in communion. They are sung on the road, around the evening campfire, and at the watering places where we stop to be refreshed. Our souls need these songs as much as our bodies need that water. They give us strength; they replenish our hearts' spent energies.

Where are we going?

PSALM 124

If the LORD had not been on our side—
let Israel say—
if the LORD had not been on our side
when men attacked us,
when their anger flared against us,

North American Protestants often seem to know and care little about the great Christian heroes (saints) who have walked the pilgrim path before us. Is that true of you?

they would have swallowed us alive;
the flood would have engulfed us,
the torrent would have swept over us,
the raging waters would have swept us away.

Praise be to the LORD,
who has not let us be torn by their teeth.
We have escaped like a bird
out of the fowler's snare;
the snare has been broken,
and we have escaped.
Our help is in the name of the Lord,
the Maker of heaven and earth.

It is no accident that the first traveling song is a song of memory. The path we walk is not a new one, unchartered and unknown. God himself first traced it, guiding the first travelers with a pillar of fire and a cloud of smoke. God fed and watered them along the way. The sign posted on the way says, Remember!

From the beginning, God told us to remember (Ex. 12:14). Our memory of the place from which we have come, of the place toward which we travel, and of who walks along with us keeps us on the road.

There are two great destroyers of memory—luxury and grief. Luxury anesthetizes memory and puts it to sleep; grief assaults memory and refuses to let it speak.

As Israel stood ready to enter Canaan and take possession of the land, the Lord spoke a word to her. Knowing that Israel's poverty would soon be over and that luxury could quickly possess her, the Lord said: Remember!

"Be careful that you do not forget the LORD, who brought you out of Egypt, out of the land of slavery" (Deut. 6:12). Remember!

"Remember how the LORD your God led you all the way in the desert . . ." (Deut. 8:2). Remember!

"When you have eaten and are satisfied, praise the LORD your God for the good land he has given you. Be careful that you do not forget the LORD your God . . . . Otherwise, when you eat and are satisfied, when you build fine houses and settle down, and when your herds and flocks grow large and your silver and gold increase and all you have is multiplied, then your heart will become proud and you will forget the Lord your God . . ." (Deut. 8:10-14). Remember!

Your traditions are the sum of what God did for your ancestors. Do you remember them with thanks or discard them as useless baggage?

■

The fruit of luxury is pride, and pride is poisonous to our memory.

The Old Testament saints needed to remember two events in order to stay on the road with and to God: the exodus and the exile. In these events, the Lord had freed the people from slavery and from sin. These were difficult to remember because both required humility and gratitude. But humility and gratitude are needed to keep us advancing on the way.

"We were slaves of Pharaoh in Egypt," the Israelite father would say to his son, "but the LORD brought us out . . . with a mighty hand" (Deut. 6:21). Humility and gratitude.

Can true gratitude exist without real humility?

■

"If the Lord had not been on our side . . . our enemies would have swallowed us alive, the floods would have engulfed us, the torrent swept over us . . ." (author's translation). This "if" leads us to confession and acknowledgment and sets us squarely on the road that leads to God. This "if" reminds us who we were and who we now are and whom we must thank for the change. This "if" keeps our hearts free from pride and our eyes on the Lord.

"If the Lord had not been merciful . . ." "If the Lord had not sent us his Son . . ." "If the Holy Spirit had not opened my eyes . . ."

This "if" comes before "Praise be to the Lord" (v. 6). We would not praise the Lord without the memory that the "if" pulls into our minds. And without it we would never declare: "Our help is in the name of the Lord, the Maker of heaven and earth" (v. 8). The memory of God's saving goodness gives rise to free and grateful praise which, in turn, enables us to rest in the assurance that the Lord will help us still today.

The earlier "my help . . ." (Ps. 121:2) has now been buttressed and nourished by the faith of the saints around us. One "my help" joined to others has grown luxuriantly into "our help . . ." (Ps. 124:8).

PSALM 125

Those who trust in the LORD are like Mount Zion,
which cannot be shaken but endures forever.
As the mountains surround Jerusalem,
so the LORD surrounds his people both now and forevermore.

The scepter of the wicked will not remain
over the land allotted to the righteous,
for then the righteous might use their hands to do evil.

Do good, O LORD, to those who are good,
to those who are upright in heart.
But those who turn to crooked ways
the LORD will banish with the evildoers.

Peace be upon Israel.

Robert Bellah writes, "the notion that one discovers one's deepest beliefs in, and through, tradition and community is not very congenial to Americans. Most of us imagine an autonomous self existing independently, entirely outside any tradition and community, and then perhaps choosing one" (*Habits of the Heart*, p. 65).

PSALM 126

When the LORD brought back the captives to Zion,
we were like men who dreamed.
Our mouths were filled with laughter,
our tongues with songs of joy.
Then it was said among the nations,
"The Lord has done great things for them."
The Lord had done great things for us,
and we are filled with joy.

Restore our fortunes, O LORD,
like streams in the Negev.
Those who sow in tears
will reap with songs of joy.
He who goes out weeping,
carrying seed to sow,
will return with songs of joy,
carrying sheaves with him.

The second Old Testament event that the communion of saints had to remember was the exile. Not the going into exile so much (although that too, of course), but the coming back from exile.

What a remarkably gracious gap exists between Psalms 125 and 126. How right it would have been to have inserted a long and detailed psalm that told how the Lord had been forgotten, how Israel's trust had shifted from the Lord's gracious presence to her own abilities and strengths, and how—when Israel once again was vulnerable without the Lord on her side—the floods, torrents, and raging waters had returned. How proper it would have been to have included here a psalm telling how the borders were crossed, the countryside overrun, the walls of Jerusalem breached, the Temple razed, and the people taken away. How just it would have seemed to have placed one last and final judgment psalm here.

Instead we have Psalm 126, a song of heartfelt, gracious laughter. The going into exile (the sin and the shame of that!) is not remembered but the Lord's leading his sinful people back (the forgiveness and the mercy in that!) is. Remember? "When the Lord brought back the captives to Zion, we were like men who dreamed. Our mouths were filled with laughter, our tongues with songs of joy."

Luxury anesthetizes memory and puts it to sleep; grief assaults memory and refuses to let it speak. In both cases, help is found in memory.

Abraham and Sarah were barren, dried up branches on an old, old tree (Gen. 11:1-30). They were a husband (one hundred years old) and wife (ninety years old) with a past but no future. They had no land and no descendants, had nothing but a fading memory of a promise God had made long before.

But then they laughed. Remember? They were given a son in their old age, a son they named "laughter," for the Lord did not forget but instead fulfilled his promise.

"By the rivers of Babylon we sat and wept . . ." (Ps. 137:1). Driven from the promised land, the people of God were overwhelmed by their sin and their punishment. But suddenly it was over, and their mouths were filled with laughter. Remember?

In confusion and in grief the women went to a tomb to honor a friend and a Lord they thought was dead. But at that place of mourning they were met by divine memory shakers. "Why do you look for the living among the dead?" they asked. "He is not here; he has risen! Remember how he told you . . . . Then they remembered . . ." (Luke 24:4-8).

Grief so quickly assaults our memory, overwhelms it, and refuses to let it speak. That is one reason why God has us travel in the communion of saints, for then those who grieve and therefore forget can be reminded that the Lord is faithful. The Lord remembers and does what he promised. We say this truth to one another: "Those who sow in tears will reap with songs of joy" (verse 5). "Weeping may remain for a night, but rejoicing comes in the morning" (Ps. 30:5).

Remember experiences of laughter during your own spiritual journey. Were they alone or with others?

PSALM 127

Unless the LORD builds the house,
its builders labor in vain.
Unless the LORD watches over the city,
the watchmen stand guard in vain.
In vain you rise early
and stay up late,
toiling for food to eat—
for he grants sleep to those he loves.

Sons are a heritage from the LORD,
children a reward from him.
Like arrows in the hands of a warrior
are sons born in one's youth.
Blessed is the man
whose quiver is full of them.
They will not be put to shame
when they contend with their enemies in the gate.

When the Lord brought the captives back to Zion, they may have laughed, but then they had to roll up their sleeves and rebuild the city. When we have suffered the consequences of our sin, we rejoice in our Lord's forgiveness and salvation, but then we must roll up our hearts and wills and rebuild our lives.

We pilgrims don't mind recalling past sins. But we refuse to dwell on them, for they have been forgiven; we have no right to give them new life. Still we need a constant reminder that without the Lord watching over the city, over our homes, and over our lives, we have no sure defense.

The city of Zion was destroyed when the Lord abandoned it because its sin had become intolerable (Ezek.

8:6; 10:18-19; 12:23). We know—yet need to remember—that sin is destructive, so any rebuilding we undertake must be done with the Lord.

"Everyone who hears these words of mine and puts them into practice is like a wise man who built his house on the rock. The rain came down, the streams rose, and the wind blew and beat against the house; yet it did not fall because it had its foundation on the rock" (Matt. 7:24-25).

Storms expose the weaknesses of every structure, which is why we pilgrims remind one another that only rebuilding done with the Lord's help will stand.

"Certainly life is not made soft for Christians but it *is*, in the last resort, safe" (Evelyn Underhill, *Anthology of the Love of God*, p. 61). Have you experienced this?

PSALM 128

Blessed are all who fear the LORD,
who walk in his ways.
You will eat the fruit of your labor;
blessings and prosperity will be yours.
Your wife will be like a fruitful vine
within your house;
your sons will be like olive shoots
around your table.
Thus is the man blessed
who fears the LORD.

May the LORD *bless you from Zion*
all the days of your life;
may you see the prosperity of Jerusalem
and may you live to see your children's children.

Peace be upon Israel.

When we give God permission to build our lives, we end up blessed. We can end no other way.

"Blessed are all who fear the LORD," the psalmist declares, "who walk in his ways." To fear the Lord is to recognize his authority, power, and good will. Recognizing these qualities of the Lord, we place our wills at his disposal and "walk in his ways."

We must recognize and say to the Lord, "he serves you best who is not so anxious to hear from you what he wills as to will what he hears from you" (Augustine, from Evelyn Underhill, *The Ways of the Spirit*).

The life, the family, or the nation that is truly formed and fashioned by the Lord is blessed. Our own sins, the sins of our spouses, and the evil resident in our political and economic structures seek to destroy what our Lord builds. But when we let him, the Lord builds only blessed lives.

For our pilgrim brothers of ancient times, the blessed life was "eating the fruit of one's labor," having a wife "like a fruitful vine," and sons who, like strong olive shoots, promise to become prized trees. In Christ, the blessing has been extended but is still wonderfully simple. Our pilgrim companions are now sisters as well as brothers, our spouses are also companions, and our daughters and sons alike are gifts from God. To have work that bears fruit that we and others can enjoy is still one of our deepest satisfactions.

Sitting around the campfire, walking together on the way, we pilgrims remember how God saved us; we encourage one another; and we testify to the goodness of the Lord.

How much of your spiritual growth comes not from your own efforts but from your no longer resisting the Spirit of God working in you?

What do we say to God?

> *We give thanks to you, O Lord our God, for all your servants and witnesses of time past: for Abraham, the father of believers, and Sarah his wife; for Moses, the lawgiver, and Aaron, the priest; for Miriam and Joshua, Deborah and Gideon, and Samuel with Hannah his mother; for Isaiah and all the prophets; for Mary, the mother of our Lord; for Peter and Paul and all the apostles; for Mary and Martha, and Mary Magdalene; for Stephen, the first martyr, and all the martyrs and saints in every age and in every land. In your mercy, O*

Lord our God, give us, as you gave to them, the hope of salvation and the promise of eternal life; through Jesus Christ our Lord, the first-born of many from the dead. Amen.

Book of Common Prayer

Join in this prayer. Continue with prayers of thanks for all those saints, past and present, who have witnessed to you and helped you on your pilgrimage.

What do we do next?

The next session deals with the dangers we encounter on the pilgrim path. Read Psalms 129, 130, and 131 in preparation. As you read and meditate on these psalms, consider the dangers of which they speak.

If the Divine call does not make us better, it will make us very much worse.
C. S. Lewis, *Reflections on the Psalms*, p. 32.

SESSION 5

DANGERS

Where are we?

"In the year that King Uzziah died, I saw the Lord . . . . Above him were seraphs . . . calling to one another: "Holy, holy, holy is the LORD Almighty; the whole earth is full of his glory." At the sound of their voices the doorposts and thresholds shook and the temple was filled with smoke. "Woe to me!" I cried. "I am ruined! For I am a man of unclean lips . . .and my eyes have seen the King, the LORD Almighty."
Isaiah 6:1-5

Have you ever trembled in awe before the holiness of God? Or do you consider such feelings inappropriate for those who have become adopted children of the Heavenly Father through Jesus Christ?

Where are we going?

PSALM 129

They have greatly oppressed me from my youth—
let Israel say—
they have greatly oppressed me from my youth,
but they have not gained the victory over me.
Plowmen have plowed my back
and made their furrows long.
But the LORD is righteous;
he has cut me free from the cords of the wicked.

May all who hate Zion
be turned back in shame.
May they be like grass on the roof,
which withers before it can grow;
with it the reaper cannot fill his hands,
nor the one who gathers fill his arms.
May those who pass by not say,
"The blessing of the LORD be upon you:
we bless you in the name of the LORD."

This is one of several psalms that makes us Christians uncomfortable. It is in the Bible and so must be taken seriously. But its fragrance is not Christ-like; its expressions are not lovely. This psalm, without embarrassment, calls down a curse on Israel's enemies. The embarrassment is ours. We wonder what to make of it.

Psalm 129 is particularly disturbing because it is meant to be sung by pilgrims on their way to the presence of God. These pilgrims had begun the journey well. Already they had traveled a good distance. Then this psalm interrupts the march and threatens its good conclusion.

By content, Psalm 129 doesn't seem to belong in this collection of the *Songs of Ascents*—yet here it is. The lips of pilgrims getting this close to God's presence should not say these words—but they do. Why? What accounts for Psalm 129?

Our sin. Our arrogance. Our pride. "God, I thank you that I am not like all other men—robbers, evildoers, adulterers . . . . I fast twice a week and I give a tenth of all I get" (Luke 18:11-12). So the Pharisee prayed about himself.

Each preceding psalm began by focusing our attention on God. We looked to him, addressed him, rejoiced in him, and encouraged others to fear the Lord. Our gaze was always on God.

Psalm 129, however, turns our eyes away from God and directs them to other people. Our oppressors, the "plowmen" and "the wicked," receive our attention here. Those who have been against us now receive our gaze—and our curse.

Gratitude to God for delivering us from our enemies (Psalm 124) is here replaced by a call for God to punish them. We have assumed a divine prerogative and pronounced judgment. The publican has turned Pharisee. How often and how easily that happens to us.

Do you agree that asking God to punish the wicked is inappropriate for a Christian?

■

The first temptation to which we humans succumbed appealed to our pride ("you will be like God," Gen. 3:5). All subsequent temptations are simply variations of that original appeal; all vices follow from it. Pride can become a great temptation to pilgrims also.

In *Reflections on the Psalms*, C. S. Lewis wrote that "the Supernatural, entering a human soul, opens to it new possibilities both of good and evil. From that point the road branches: one way to sanctity, love and humility, the other to spiritual pride, self-righteousness, persecuting zeal" (pp. 31-32).

Psalm 129 is an expression of that second branch. It is good that we notice the fact that even after we have begun our journey to the presence of God, this other way still branches off and beckons to us. It can take us very far away from God.

In the case of some sins, we are deceived by the world. The entrance to our souls is unguarded, and these sins enter and quickly overwhelm us. In the case of pride, we deceive ourselves. We tell ourselves the lie of our own goodness, and we listen to ourselves. We agree with what we say.

"All a man's ways seem right to him . . ." (Prov. 21:2). It's the ways of others that seem so wrong! As Matthew put it, "Why do you look at the speck of sawdust that is in your brother's eye and pay no attention to the plank in your own eye?" (7:3). Why indeed!

What do you think of this statement by C. S. Lewis? Have you experienced the temptations of this other way on your spiritual journey?

PSALM 130

Out of the depths I cry to you, O LORD;
O Lord, hear my voice.
Let your ears be attentive
to my cry for mercy.

If you, O LORD, kept a record of sins,
O Lord, who could stand?
But with you there is forgiveness;
therefore you are feared.

I wait for the LORD, my soul waits,
and in his word I put my hope.
My soul waits for the Lord
more than watchmen wait for the morning,
more than watchmen wait for the morning.

O Israel, put your hope in the LORD,
for with the LORD is unfailing love
and with him is full redemption.
He himself will redeem Israel
from all their sins.

If this psalm were not here, our journey would have ended without our reaching our destination. Psalm 129 would have ended our pilgrimage, for only the pure in heart will see God (Matt. 5:8). Pride has made our hearts impure, and there is only one way for them to be cleansed—by our repentance and God's forgiveness.

Out of the depths! *De profundis* in Latin. What miracle occurred here? After Psalm 129 drew the pilgrim into the depths, how did he come to understand so clearly where he was? What divine miracle enables us to see the great gulf that pride places between us and God?

De profundis! Through God's grace and love, once again our eyes are where they belong—on God. "Out of the depths I cry to you, O Lord . . . ."

Our journey began with the cry, "Woe to me that I dwell in Meshech, that I live among the tents of Kedar!" Distress that life was being lived far from God set us off on our pilgrimage. But that "woe" is not nearly as acute as this anguished cry from out of the depths. *De profundis!*

No journey to God's presence should be expected to go smoothly or be easy. Forces without wait to ambush us; forces within seek to halt our progress. Of the two, the forces within are the more difficult and necessary to overcome.

"Out of the depths I cry to you, O Lord; O Lord, hear my voice!" Our journey has changed profoundly now. We were much in charge before. We took the first steps; we joined other travelers; we remembered with them how good our God has been to us. Our pilgrimage was advancing nicely; God was with us and we were with God.

But how different now. We are in the depths. Our enemies haven't put us here. No physical illness or sudden accident threw us here. We descended to the depths ourselves, precipitously, driven down by our pride.

Here in the depths our relationship with the Lord, toward whom we were so comfortably moving, is abruptly different. For we cannot move forward at all anymore. We are in the depths, and all we can do is cry out. All we can do is pray that the Lord will hear us, be merciful, and pull us up.

Is every spiritual pilgrimage halted by such an "in the depths" experience? Can a group of pilgrims experience this, or only individuals?

■

That such a cry is necessary is due to our failings. That such a cry is possible is based on an extraordinary assertion, one that would seem only a human dream if it were not also a revealed truth. "If you, O Lord, kept a record of sins . . . who could stand?"

That's the first part of this assertion. If God remembered every insult, every act of rebellion, every word spoken against someone or something he loved, there would be no way out of the depths we are in and no escape from a just condemnation. If God kept a record of our sins against him as assiduously as we record the sins committed against us, we would be stuck in the deepest despair.

"But with you there is forgiveness." Here's the second part. Out of the depths we look up to God and see that the divine nature is not to record our sins but to forgive them. From the depths we look up and see a God who wants to lift us up.

This is the gospel. This is the apostle Paul in Old Testament robes. This is the incarnate Word whispered to us. "But with you there is forgiveness!" This is our hope and our salvation.

Out of the depths we cry to our Lord. To whom else can we cry? From the depths we look up and see that with God there is forgiveness (v. 4), steadfast love, and full redemption (v. 7). Therefore we wait for him and put our hope in his word. Waiting for him is all we can do.

Waiting for God is what we must do. As the watchman waits in the darkness for morning to come, we wait in the depths for the Lord to pull us out. As the watchman waits knowing that the morning certainly will come, so we wait knowing that our Lord does forgive, that his love will not fail us, and that our redemption is near.

Do you think of God as forgiving you eagerly or reluctantly? On what do you base your view?

PSALM 131

My heart is not proud, O LORD,
my eyes are not haughty;
I do not concern myself with great matters
or things too wonderful for me.
But I have stilled and quieted my soul,
like a weaned child with its mother,
like a weaned child is my soul within me.

O Israel, put your hope in the LORD
both now and forevermore.

Our journey is now forever different. We might think of it as starting over, as now truly beginning. We sinned and had to be forgiven. We wandered far off course and had to be pulled back onto the path. We cannot be arrogant pilgrims anymore. Pride was cut away from us and now, as children, we move ahead. We cannot advance now unless we do so as children: "I tell you the truth, unless you change and become like little children, you will never enter the kingdom of heaven" (Matt. 18:3).

There are, in truth, no adult Christians, only childlike followers of Jesus. The greatest saints are those among us who have become most childlike.

"My heart is not proud, O LORD." After the last two psalms our hearts cannot be proud. Psalm 130 pulls us through the pride of Psalm 129 and leads us into the humility of Psalm 131.

When a child in the middle of Jesus' disciples, Jesus did not say to that child, "Grow up and become like the adults around you." Instead, Jesus said to us, his disciples, "Become like this child." Children don't have to grow up in order to enter the kingdom of heaven; we adults have to grow down.

Growing down is not easy. Growing up means deciding matters for ourselves, creating our own destinies, structuring things, and placing people where they fit our designs. Growing down means allowing God to decide all such matters, handing over our destinies to him, placing all our things and all our people into the structures of his reality.

■

"Like a weaned child with its mother, like a weaned child is my soul within me."

Every mother knows the difference between a child that is not weaned and one that finally is. A baby still breastfeeding is a demanding baby. He knows only his immediate need and insists that it be met. He is hungry, so he cries out, and his mother is there to satisfy him.

In *Gravity and Grace,* Simone Weil said, "God allows me to exist outside himself. It is for me to refuse this authorization. Humility is the refusal to exist outside God" (p. 35). Is this true?

The relationship between an unweaned child and her mother is one of unilateral dependence. Given the biological circumstances, that relationship is necessary. But it is not meant to be permanent. It must be temporary, for the good of the child and of her mother. Every child must be weaned. That doesn't make her less of a child, but it develops and enriches the relationship between child and mother.

A weaned child no longer exclusively takes; a weaned child responds, trusts, loves, and brings us so much pleasure.

There are times when, in our desperate need, we cry out to our Lord, as children cry. Often he comes and answers our cries, rescuing us from the traps that have ensnared us.

But although God wants us to be his children, he wants us to be weaned. So sometimes he doesn't answer so directly. Our Lord doesn't want us to be neurotically dependent, seeking him only for saving help. We must be weaned. God wants us to love him for his own sake and out of our own desire. Of course God helps us. But sometimes that help comes from a distance. It's a word instead of a hand, a smile of encouragement rather than a miracle of deliverance.

Therefore our Lord might withhold a few things from us, might allow difficult circumstances to continue, or might delay responding to our cries. This is not because God has grown indifferent to us but because he wants us weaned. For when we are weaned, we can love rather than simply need him. When we are weaned, we can hold his hand, and run with and pull that hand in our childlike enthusiasm, all the while knowing that God keeps us on the path.

Can you think of any examples of people (perhaps you yourself at some stage of your own journey) who have been neurotically dependent on God? How did that dependence show itself?

What do we say to God?

Thou hast given so much to me
Give one thing more—a grateful heart:
Not thankful when it pleaseth me,
As if Thy blessings had spare days,
But such a heart whose pulse may be
Thy praise.

George Herbert, in Evelyn Underhill,
The Ways of the Spirit, p. 64

Using this prayer to begin, join in expressing your gratitude to God for all his blessings.

What do we do next?

The next session will be your last with these materials. Read and meditate on Psalms 132, 133, and 134. Feel something of the intense joy that the Israelites experienced as their pilgrimage brought them to Zion, the dwelling place of the Lord.

Since I am coming to that holy room, where, with thy choir of saints for evermore,
I shall be made thy music; as I come I tune the instrument here at the door,
And what I must do then, think here before.

John Donne, "Hymn to God, my God, in my sickness"

SESSION 6

ARRIVAL

Where are we?

St. Ignatius makes one principle the foundation of his exercises: "The human being was created for *this* end—to praise, reverence, and serve the Lord." Because that sounds all right, it slips by, like so many religious phrases, almost unchecked. But if we stop and look at it and at the chosen order of his terms, what does it mean?

Praise—Reverence—Service. Our first duty is adoration, then awe, and finally, service. For those three things and nothing else, addressed to God and to no one else, *you*, says Ignatius, were created. Two of the three things for which your soul was made are matters of attitude and relationship. Unless those two are right, the last will not be right. Unless the whole of life is a movement of praise and adoration, unless instinct combines with awe, your work will not be of much value.

Evelyn Underhill, *The Ways of the Spirit*, p. 111

■

Of praise, reverence, and service, which is most central to your life? To your church? Are they balanced?

Unexpectedly, our journey now slows and becomes deliberate. Our goal is in sight and, if it were a destination other than the presence of the Almighty One, we might hurry now and speed our steps to arrive more quickly. But we are slowed by the awareness of whom we are about to meet. God awaits us, and it is best for us to take considered steps. Psalms 132, 133, and 134 measure our approach to God. They give us time to tune our instruments.

PSALM 132

O LORD, remember David
and all the hardships he endured.

He swore an oath to the LORD
and made a vow to the Mighty One of Jacob:
"I will not enter my house
or go to my bed—
I will allow no sleep to my eyes
no slumber to my eyelids,
till I find a place for the LORD,
a dwelling for the Mighty One of Jacob."

We heard it in Ephrathah,
we came upon it in the fields of Jaar:
"Let us go to his dwelling place;
let us worship at his footstool—
arise, O LORD, and come to your resting place,
you and the ark of your might.
May your priests be clothed with righteousness;
may your saints sing for joy."

For the sake of David your servant,
do not reject your anointed one.

The LORD swore an oath to David,
a sure oath that he will not revoke:
"One of your own descendants
I will place on your throne—
If your sons keep my covenant
and the statutes I teach them,
then their sons will sit
on your throne for ever and ever."

For the LORD has chosen Zion,
he has desired it for his dwelling:
"This is my resting place for ever and ever;
here I will sit enthroned, for I have desired it—
I will bless her with abundant provisions;
her poor will I satisfy with food.

For a few moments, think silently about this introductory statement.

I will clothe her priests with salvation,
and her saints will ever sing for joy.

"Here I will make a horn grow for David
and set up a lamp for my anointed one.
I will clothe his enemies with shame,
but the crown on his head will be resplendent."

This psalm brings the coming encounter into sharp focus. It relates what we are to do: "Let us go to his dwelling place; let us worship at his footstool" (v. 7). It prays that God will do what he must do: "Arise, O LORD, and come to your resting place" (v. 8). Two wills, ours and God's, must be exercised if this encounter is to take place.

"Will God really dwell on earth?" Solomon asked for us all. "The heavens, even the highest heavens, cannot contain you. How much less this temple I have built" (1 Kings 8:27).

If God is to meet us, he must arise and come. Coming, he must make himself small, speak in simple sentences, cover our sins, forgive our fidgeting, and listen to music we like—and presume God likes too. If God is to meet us, he must leave his glory and step down—far down—to our streets, to our churches, to our company.

If we are to meet God we must go and worship at his footstool.

Of the two, God's will is exercised most, and surely most willingly. "I have consecrated this temple, which you have built, by putting my Name there forever. My eyes and my heart will always be there" (1 Kings 9:3). God is forever ready to be worshiped.

If we are to meet God, we must go and worship at his footstool. Going requires that we give up our time; worship demands that we give up our hearts. The former calls for our decision; the latter for our preparation.

In years past, shoes were shined, dresses and shirts ironed, cinnamon rolls made on Saturday night so that Sunday morning we would be prepared to worship. Christians avoided late travel or Saturday night parties, for there was worship next morning and we had to be prepared.

■

Psalm 132 calls us to go and worship. The actual worship won't occur until Psalm 135, but our instruments must be tuned before the symphony begins to play. Consider these ideas:

- "Clearly, the meaning of one's life for most Americans is to become one's own person, almost to give birth to oneself" (Robert Bellah, *Habits of the Heart*, p. 82).
- True Christian worship is "the one little human spirit's humble adoring acknowledgment of the measureless glory of God . . ." (E. Underhill, *Collected Papers*, p. 66).

If these two thoughts are correct, we have a great deal of preparation to do before we can worship, for God must be the focus of our hearts and the object of our desire. We must lose ourselves so that we may find him, for God is all that matters in worship. Before God, the *sanctus* ("Holy, holy, holy is the Lord God Almighty, who was, and is, and is to come," Rev. 4:8) is our only norm, and the *dignus* ("Worthy is the Lamb who was slain, to receive power and wealth and wisdom and strength and honor and glory and praise," Rev. 5:12) is our greatest song.

Did your family prepare for worship in the way described here? How do you (and your family) usually prepare for worship today?

Describe the things you ideally should do to prepare for worship.

PSALM 133

How good and pleasant it is
when brothers live together in unity!
It is like precious oil poured on the head,
running down on the beard,

running down on Aaron's beard,
down upon the collar of his robes.
It is as if the dew of Hermon
were falling on Mount Zion.
For there the L*ORD* *bestows his blessing,*
even life forevermore.

We began our journey to the presence of God alone, our souls individually awakened by the touch of God's Spirit. But soon we were asked to join other travelers (by God as well as by these others) and to become part of a company of like-hearted pilgrims journeying along the way.

Now, arriving at the place where God dwells, we look around us at those fellow pilgrims. They are so many and so different; Jew and Gentile, male and female, black and white. So much distinguishes and separates us from them; so much makes and keeps us strangers to each other. And yet we know that among pilgrims there are no strangers.

How good it is when brothers and sisters of every nation, every race, and every class dwell together in unity! How pleasant it is when the unity is free, unforced, spontaneous. How good and pleasant when the pilgrims together gaze upon the goodness, majesty, and beauty of the Lord. As A. W. Tozer noted, "A hundred pianos all tuned to the same fork are automatically tuned to each other" (*The Pursuit of God*, p. 96).

Have you ever worshiped with people of other ethnic or social backgrounds, or of other nations? Did you find that experience especially good and pleasant?

■

"If you are offering your gifts at the altar and there remember that your brother has something against you, leave your gift there in front of the altar. First go and be reconciled to your brother, then come . . ." (Matt. 5:23-24).

We cannot ask for peace with God if we have provoked war with others. We must prepare for worship by reconciling ourselves with those we have offended.

What a blessing that unity turns out to be! When we dwell in godly unity, life is like precious sweet-smelling perfume that gives the entire body a fresh and invigorating scent, like morning-fresh dew watering the grass and the flowers. The Lord sends his blessing there.

Have you ever gone and talked with someone you had offended or who had offended you? Did that result in a blessing?

PSALM 134

Praise the LORD, all you servants of the LORD
who minister by night in the house of the LORD.
Lift up your hands in the sanctuary
and praise the LORD.

May the LORD, the Maker of heaven and earth,
bless you from Zion.

This is the last of the *Songs of Ascents* and the final psalm of our journey. Think of it as the last rehearsal and final tuning of our instruments before we play in the presence of our God.

Our journey began in great distress. We recognized that we were so far from God. We saw ourselves surrounded by people of "lying lips" and "deceitful tongues," and by destroyers of peace and lovers of war (Psalm 120).

Now we are surrounded by brothers and sisters, enjoying a good and pleasant unity. Now we receive blessings from our Lord. From distress to blessing, we have traveled far.

Early in our journey we looked up to the hills, apprehensive about the way but reassuring ourselves that our help would come from "the Lord, the Maker of heaven and earth" (Psalm 121).

Our help came from him indeed! We look back and acknowledge it with deep gratitude. All along the way and at life's every stage, our help came from the Lord. And now, as we prepare to go into his presence, as we stand ready to face him . . . the Lord blesses us! "May the LORD, the Maker of heaven and earth, bless you . . . ."

The sounds, the acts, the sweet aroma of blessing are everywhere in Psalm 134. The servants of the Lord bless him (vv. 1-2). He blesses them and through them he blesses us. Blessings here go around and around, from God to us and to God from us . . . . "Praise be to the God and Father of our Lord Jesus Christ, who has blessed us with every spiritual blessing . . ." (Eph. 1:3).

Before we get a chance to say anything to God, we receive his blessing!

Do you ever bless God? Do you think of blessing as an exchange between God and yourself? What does it mean to you to be blessed by God?

PSALM 135:1-4

Praise the LORD.

Praise the name of the LORD;
praise him, you servants of the LORD,
you who minister in the house of the LORD,
in the courts of the house of our God.

Praise the LORD, for the LORD is good;
sing praise to his name, for that is pleasant.
For the LORD has chosen Jacob to be his own,
Israel to be his treasured possession.

C. S. Lewis wrote that "if it were possible . . . to love and delight in the worthiest object of all and simultaneously at every moment to give this delight perfect expression, then [we] would be in supreme beatitude" (*Reflections on the Psalms*, p. 96). Then we would be engaging in true and pure worship.

We have now arrived and, in the presence of God, one thing only fills our hearts and is on our lips: praise. Praise and praise and more praises still. You and I who have recently come, all the saints already here, angels, and creatures of every kind praise the Lord. For we see that "the Lord is good" (v. 3).

Why is our Lord's goodness the first thing that evokes the psalmist's (and our) praise? Because we are creatures of the earth and are in the presence of the Lord. Our being in his presence is solely due to his goodness.

God's justice would not have us here. God's holiness would keep us away. But his goodness allows us to come; the Lord's goodness permits us to stay. "Praise the Lord, for the Lord is good!"

"Then Moses said, 'Now show me your glory!' And the Lord said, 'I will cause all my goodness to pass in front of you . . .'" (Ex. 33:18-19). God's glory, that which brings him honor, that which makes him unique in heaven and on earth, is his goodness.

Of what does his goodness consist? "Then he [the Lord] passed in front of Moses, proclaiming, 'The LORD, the LORD, the compassionate and gracious God, slow to anger, abounding in steadfast love and faithfulness, maintaining love to thousands, and forgiving wickedness, rebellion and sin'" (Ex. 34:6-7).

God's glory is his goodness, and his goodness is our salvation. "Praise the Lord, for the Lord is good . . . ." Here on earth we praise him for his goodness that even now we see. But when we shall see him face to face, then the height, the depth, the width, and the length of his goodness will be fully viewed. We will then know how good our Lord truly is and our praise will be full-throated. It can't be anything less, for the Lord is good!

He is also great (Ps. 135:5). "'I am a great King!' says the LORD Almighty, 'and my name is to be feared among the nations'" (Mal. 1:14). Greater than all gods (Ps. 135:5), master of nature (vv. 6-7), sovereign director of history (vv. 8-14), our Lord's greatness exposes all other gods to be idols made in the image of men (vv. 15-18).

The prophet Daniel once had a nightmare in which he saw four horrible beasts, each one more terrifying than the other. They were our rulers, the human kingdoms set up by us, for us, and over us. But they crushed us, devoured us, and brought death upon us.

Then the nightmare turned into a dream. "I looked, and there before me was one like a son of man, coming with the clouds of heaven. He approached the Ancient of Days and was led into his presence. He was given authority, glory and sovereign power; all peoples, nations and men of every language worshiped him. His dominion is an everlasting dominion that will not pass away, and his kingdom is one that will never be destroyed" (Dan. 7:13-14).

> *"O house of Israel, praise the LORD;*
> *O house of Aaron, praise the LORD;*
> *O house of Levi, praise the LORD;*
> *you who fear him, praise the LORD.*
> *Praise be to the Lord from Zion,*
> *to him who dwells in Jerusalem.*
> *Praise the Lord."*
>
> Psalm 135:19-21

Do you think this statement by C. S. Lewis is a good description of real and perfect worship? Have you ever experienced such worship?

What do we say to God?

> *"O Lord, in whom all things live, who commands us to seek you, and are ever ready to be found: to know you is life, to serve you is freedom, to praise you is our souls' joy. We bless you and adore you, we worship you and magnify you, we give thanks to you for your great glory; through Jesus Christ our Lord."*
>
> St. Augustine (from Evelyn Underhill, *The Ways of the Spirit*, p. 105)

Close the session and the study of the *Songs of Ascents* with Augustine's prayer and with your own, dedicated to praising God for his goodness.